Siamese Cats

Siamese
Cats

Mary Dunnill

Colour photography by
Paddy Cutts/Animals Unlimited

B. T. Batsford Ltd., London

Frontispiece Sumfun
Soraya with her kittens
— these are
Sealpoints.

ISBN 0 7134 4103 8

Typeset by Typewise Limited, Wembley, Middlesex
and printed in Hong Kong
for the publishers
B. T. Batsford Ltd
4 Fitzhardinge Street
London W1H 0AH

Contents

1 The Early History of the Siamese

The origin of the Siamese cat is lost in antiquity but it is generally accepted that the Siamese is of Eastern origin, perhaps brought from China along the old trading routes. In the National Library in Bangkok are manuscripts saved from Ayudha, the ancient capital of Siam, one of which records the native cats of the time. *Cat-Book Poems* shows a pale-coated cat with a black tail, feet and ears, surely a sealpoint Siamese. Since Ayudha was founded in 1350, there must have been pointed cats by that date.

The naturalist Peter Simon Pallas, journeying in Russia in 1793, describes in the book of his travels three domestic cats he observed showing the Siamese coat pattern – light brown bodies with dark points. A black cat had kittened and produced three young ones which exactly resembled each other. Pallas describes one of them as follows:

It is of middle size, has somewhat smaller legs than the common cat, and the head is longer toward the nose. The tail is thrice the length of the head. The colour of the body is a light chestnut brown like that of a pole-cat but blacker on the back, especially towards the tail, and paler along the sides and belly. The throat is whiter and the female has a white spot on the lower part of the neck. A black streak runs along the nose, surrounds the eyes and ends in a point on the forehead. The ears, paws and tail are quite black. The hair, like that of the pole-cat, is softer than that of the common cat and the lower or furry part is of whitish grey. The hair of the tail is somewhat elastic and lies in flat divisions.

Siamese cats were little known in Europe until late last century. Occasionally they were seen in zoos, such as those in Berlin, Frankfurt and the Hague. They were first seen in England at the Crystal Palace Cat Show in 1871. Great interest was aroused in these unusual cats and many were imported. It was said that they were bred by the King of Siam and therefore the sealpoints became known as 'Palace' cats or 'Royal' Siamese. There were two kinds of Siamese among the early imports, the dun Siamese with, in Harrison Weir's words, 'body of a dun colour, nose, part of the face, ears, feet and tail of a very dark chocolate brown, nearly black, eyes of a beautiful blue by day and of a red colour at night'. The other kind was 'of a very rich chocolate or seal, with darker face, ears and tail, the legs are a shade darker which intensifies toward the feet'. The eyes were a rich amber colour. Even among the 'Royal' Siamese, there appeared to be two types, one a rather small long-headed cat with glossy close-lying coat and deep blue eyes, the other, a larger cat with a rounder head, a much thicker, longer and less close-lying coat and paler blue eyes.

In 1884, Owen Gould brought a pair of Siamese cats from Siam as a gift for his sister Lilian. These two cats, Pho and Mia, father and mother, are *1a* and *2a* in the Siamese Cat Register, but they have no 'pedigree'; their particulars are 'unknown, imported from Bangkok'. The progeny of Pho and Mia, Duen Ngai and Kalahom and Karomata were exhibited at the Crystal Palace in 1885 and swept the board, but unfortunately died after

Illustration from the *Cat Book Poems.*

7

Tiam O'Shian IV, born 15 August 1899, was a prize-winner at the Crystal Palace Shows of 1900 and 1901.

TIAM · O'SHIAN IV

Mrs Roberts Locke with Calif, Siam and Bangkok, the first two of which 'carried all before them' at the Chicago Show in 1902.

the show. Between 1884 and the end of the century, a considerable number of Siamese cats were imported into England and are recorded in the Siamese Cat Registers. Miss Forestier Walker, one of the founder Committee members of the original Siamese Cat Club, owned Tiam O'Shian who was the sire of Tiam O'Shian II, bred by Mrs Lee, of Pensford. Tiam O'Shian III was born in 1894 and was bred by Miss A. Forestier Walker and owned by her sister, Lady Vyvyan. Tiam O'Shian IV, born in 1899 and bred and owned by Lady Vyvyan, was winning prizes at the Crystal Palace shows in 1900. He was registered with the original National Cat Club. Another of the early prize-winning cats was Cuss, bred by Lady Marcus Beresford, registered with The Cat Club and winning at the Westminster Show in 1899. Presumably all these were blue-eyed Royal Siamese.

Gaywood Suhaili, Sealpoint, is 'old-fashioned' in type, but shows good contrast in the points colour. Owner Mrs Barbara Harrington.

Zenobia Baboushka, Bluepoint, owned by Mrs Jean Gamble and bred by Mrs D. Bailey. Sire: Ch Maytime Angelo; dam: Gracelands Zamandra.

Ma, Sood, Tilu, all born in 1897, Trump and litter sister Mhow born in 1899, are recorded in the Register as chocolate, presumably the golden-eyed dark-coated cats. They were either sired by, or related to, Prince of Siam. All these chocolates were bred or owned by Miss Sutherland. Ma and Tilu were passed to Lady Marcus Beresford who sent them to Mrs Clinton Locke, the 'Mother of the American Cat Fancy'. They were later passed to Mrs W. A. Hofstra, President of the Atlantic Cat Club, who became President of the Cat Fanciers' Association. These two cats ruled the American show bench for a long time and are the ancestors of many American-bred Siamese. It seems very likely that they are Netherlands Tilu and Netherlands Ma listed in Volume II of the Beresford Stud Book in the United States of America.

Mrs Clinton Locke founded the Beresford Cat Club in 1899 and was its first President. Calif and Bangkok were bred from Siam and Sally Ward and 'carried all before them' at the Chicago Show in 1902. Lockhaven Siam and Sally are the first registered Siamese cats in America recorded in Volume I of the Beresford Stud Book issued in 1900. Siam was purchased by Mrs Robert Locke in France and was the first Siamese to win a 'Best Cat' award. Frances Simpson, in *The Book of the Cat*, tells us that 'Miss Sutherland who lives in the South of France used to breed a lot of good Siamese from her imported Prince of Siam'. Perhaps all these cats had a common ancestor in Prince of Siam.

Probably the first Siamese cat in America arrived during the Presidency of Rutherford B. Hayes (1877-81) as a present from the American Consul in Bangkok to the President's wife, Mrs Lucy Webb Hayes. Mrs Hayes was notified that a Siamese cat consigned to her had arrived from Hong Kong on 3 January 1879. It was transported to the Golden Gate's port on the steam-powered SS Belgic with charges prepaid by the Consul in Bangkok. It had been placed in the charge of the ship's purser until it reached San Francisco and, thence was sent by express to Washington. It arrived safely at the White House and was named 'Siam'. She soon became a favourite and was much admired. However, in September, Siam became ill and refused offers of chicken, fish, duck, oysters, milk and cream. The White House physician took her into his own home so that he and his wife could give the cat their full attention but, in spite of their efforts, poor Siam died on 1 October 1879. This early arrival is authenticated by letters and forwarding receipts to be found in the Hayes Library and Museum, and calls into question the theory that Siamese cats were first brought to America from England in 1895. It is also earlier than the recorded date, 1884, at which the first identified pair, Pho and Mia, came to England, although we do know that Siamese cats were seen at the first official Cat Show in 1871 organized by Harrison Weir at the Crystal Palace.

In his book *Cats* published in 1892, the English writer Harrison Weir gives Points of Excellence for the Royal Cat of Siam. He says, 'light rich dun is the preferable colour, but a light fawn, light silver-gray or light orange is allowable; deeper and richer browns, almost chocolate are admissible if even and not clouded but the first is the true type, the last merely a variety of much beauty and excellence but the dun and light tints take precedence'. The Committee of the newly formed Siamese Cat Club drew up the first Standard of Points and only recognized as Siamese cats those which conformed to that standard.

Undoubtedly there were other colours among the early cats but it is not easy to know them from the various registers. There is the story of Mr Spearman's blue Siamese at the Holland House show in 1896 and Louis Wain's refusal to judge it because it was 'blue and not biscuit as were the majority of Siamese which we had seen up to that time'. This cat could very

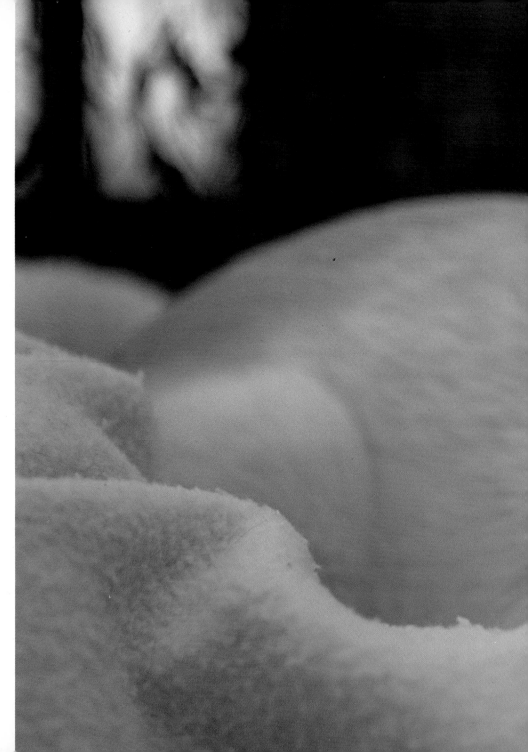

Gr Ch Pentangle Beauman, Chocolatepoint, owned by Mrs Joan Grabham, and bred by Mrs J. Walker. Sire: Gr Ch Penyrallt Picasso; dam: Chundaw Kali. Sadly now dead, he was one of the few cats with correct 'milk' chocolate, not 'plain' chocolate points.

well be Lady Blue Blue of Pegu, number 320 in the first Siamese Cat Register, 'owner Mrs Spearman'.

The Bluepoints were regarded as sports and only a handful of breeders were interested in them; very few were registered as Bluepoints. One of the earliest was Rhoda, born in 1894. Rhoda was mated to Jacob II and produced Prince, a Bluepoint and Duke of Abinger, a black. Again, mated to the same stud, she produced Princess and Menam; in the same litter were Chon Kina, a black, Topsy and Miss Abinger, colour not stated, all being females. Menam was registered with The Cat Club and won a Third prize at Westminster in 1900.

Donato was advertised at stud, 'siring kittens with good seal points (he has blue points)'. Donato's sire was Erroll and his grandsire was Carlisle Lad. His dam was Si-he who had a double dose of Carlisle Lad. Mrs Scott Russell owned Kuching Susan, a Bluepoint born in 1922, the dam of Donatina of Cornwall and Eve of Woodroffe, both Bluepoints. These two cats were exported to the United States of America.

The first Bluepoint to be registered by the Governing Council of the Cat Fancy (today's governing body in Britain, responsible ultimately for all breeds), is Gris-Nez. She was given a Fifth prize at Newbury in 1930. Carlisle Lad was one of her ancestors.

By the 1930s there was a substantial number of breeders interested in Bluepoints. Some shows put on the odd class for them but they were not allowed to enter the side classes. However, a group of enthusiasts persevered and at a meeting of the Governing Council of the Cat Fancy on 19 February 1936, the Bluepointed Siamese cat was officially recognized and granted its own breed number, 24a. Official recognition ensured that classes must be put on for Bluepoints at shows and from then onwards, Bluepoint Siamese came into their own. They have their own club and send two delegates to Council.

Chocolatepoint Siamese fared even worse than the Bluepoints when Siamese cats first came to Britain. The cats called Chocolate and recorded in the Registers as 'colour chocolate' are generally believed to be brown cats. It is open to question whether Chocolatepointed Siamese derived from an all-brown cat but it is certain that many of the imported cats carried the gene for chocolate-brown as well as the blue dilution. They were regarded as 'poor seals' and registered as Sealpoints or 'usual'.

The first cat recorded as a Chocolatepoint in a GCCF stud book is Eryx, sired by Southampton Darboy out of Baby and born in 1931. His ancestry can be traced to Carlisle Lad and Kew Prince of Siam. During the 1930s, Miss Wentworth Fitzwilliam was breeding mixed litters of Sealpoints and Chocolatepoints from Mirabelle de Listinoise who was a Chocolatepoint but registered as a Sealpoint; so, too, were her offspring. One of her descendants, Seashell de Listinoise, became the property of Mrs Kathleen Williams and was the dam of Doneraile Brun Boy. When he was shown in 1950 it was said, 'this is not a bad seal but a real chocolate at last'. Mrs Williams was exhibiting, in the same year, a litter of six 'pure chocolatepoints, probably the first all chocolate litter to be bred in the country'.

A band of enthusiasts headed by Miss E. Wentworth Fitzwilliam worked hard to achieve a proper status for the Chocolatepoints and in 1950, the Governing Council of the Cat Fancy granted them the breed number 24b. So the 'poor seals' were re-registered as 24b and classes with championship status were put on for them at the shows. Volume 10 of the Governing Council stud books lists 16 chocolatepointed Siamese and Volume II carries 43 registered Chocolatepoints. Today, they are very popular but there is a tendency for the points to be too dark, and very careful selection is necessary to ensure that they do not slip back to 'poor seals'. Chocolatepoint

Siamese have their own club and are represented in Council.

There must have been Lilacpointed Siamese cropping up in the litters bred from the early cats since we know that there were Bluepoints and Chocolatepoints. The Lilacpoint is produced by the effect of two genes for chocolate upon the Bluepoint cat or two genes for dilution upon the Chocolatepoint. There is no gene for lilac. However, as with other 'sports' and 'freaks' they would be discarded or registered as seals and therefore unidentified in the registers and stud books. Mrs P. Lauder's · Bellhaven Apple Blossom was a Lilacpoint out of a Chocolatepoint sired by a Sealpoint.

The 'experimentally' bred Lilacpoints were always referred to as hybrids. Mrs Hargreaves mated Laurentide Ludo, a Sealpoint born in 1946, with Silvershoen Blue Peter, a Russian Blue with Russian Blue parents. The first generation, self-blacks, mated to Sealpoints produced Sealpoints; two of these second generation Sealpoints mated together produced Laurentide Ephree Amethyst, born in 1951, registered and exhibited as a Bluepoint in 1952. Amethyst was mated to Chatwyn Tamarack, a Bluepoint whose dam, Mistery Maid, traces her ancestry back to the Russian Blue cross. This mating produced Laurentide Mercury who was first registered as a Bluepoint and was re-registered later as a Chocolatepoint. His breeder claimed he was a Lilacpoint and after a lot of 'hum'ing and ha'ing' from the Powers-that-be, he was registered as a Lilacpoint.

Lilacpoints were allocated the breed number 24c in 1960 in Britain. They had been officially recognized in the United States of America in 1954/5 but were called Frostpoints. The early Lilacpoints were inclined to be heavy in build but, with careful selection, they have made rapid progress and today are well represented among the Champions.

Over the years, Tabbypointed cats have made

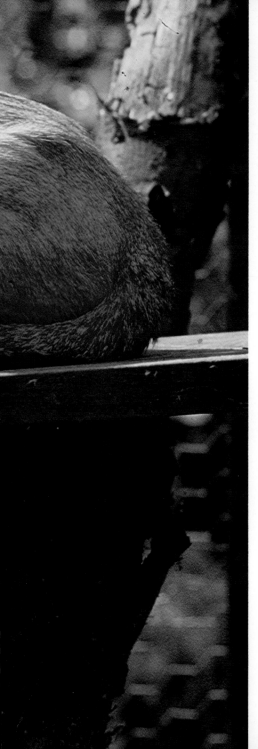

their appearance in random places. Frances Simpson mentions them in 1902. Mrs Hood was breeding them in Scotland in the 1940s, but the present day Tabbypoints, for the most part, trace their ancestry to a cat called Patti. Patti's dam was a Sealpoint queen named Lady Me who had found her own mate, presumably a tabby carrying Siamese genes. An 'unusual' kitten in the resulting litter was a female and she was named Patti. Patti was mated to Mrs M. Buttery's Samsara Saracen and out of six kittens, four were Tabbypoints. This litter was shown in 1961 and caused quite a stir. Mrs D. Hindley bought a female kitten and named her Tansy. Many beautiful Tabbypoints have her prefix Prestwick. An unrelated line stems from a half-Siamese called Tiggi who also produced these 'unusual' kittens. One of them, named Miss Tee Kat, was mated to Richard Warner's Spotlight Troubadour and produced a male Tabbypoint, Mr Buttons, who went to Miss Alexander as a mate for Patti. Praline, a female, was taken by Mr and Mrs R. Warner. These cats were the progenitors of the spectacular cats known at first as Shadowpoints or Lynxpoints. The early generations were registered as breed 26, Any Other Variety, and could only be shown in such classes. They were officially recognized as Siamese in 1966 and were given the number 32, not an extension of the breed number 24 which covers the four 'solid' colour varieties. To maintain their superb type, freedom to back-cross to good quality Siamese was necessary. Initially only Sealpoints were used but inevitably Bluepoints, Chocolatepoints and Lilacpoints have been used.

Mr and Mrs Warner's Praline, mated to Whiteoaks Malahide, produced the first two Champion Tabbypoints, Spotlight Penny Lynx and Spotlight Petit Burlinks. In 1971, Mrs A. Aslin's Champion Seremban Liger became the first Siamese cat to gain the new award of Grand Champion. Today, there are some exquisite Tabbypoints on the show bench. Grand

Ch Killdown Midas, Seal Tabbypoint, owned by Brian and Anne Gregory and bred by Mrs I. Keene. Sire: Ch Valena Beauregard; dam Killdown Poppy.

Overleaf Ch and Pr Leolee Mr Apricot, Redpoint, owned and bred by Mrs S.L. Jackson. Sire: Gr Ch Amberseal Electo; dam: Marilane Honeydew.

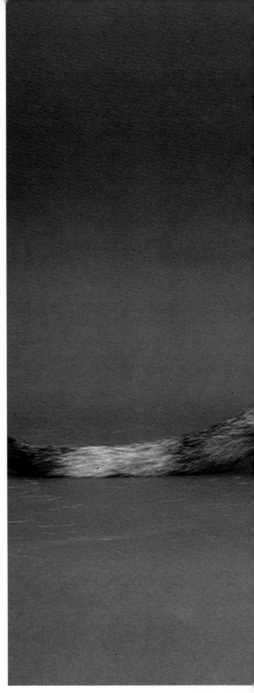

Ch Cobweb Mist, Tortiepoint, owned by Mr Peter Greenaway.
Sire: Ch Patrician Nijinsky; dam: Pascha Topsun.

Ch and Pr Palantir Tom Bombadil, Creampoint, bred and owned by Miss Julia May. Sire: Ch Coromandel Blue Beau; dam: Ch Palantir Nenya.

Champion Zachary Apollo was named the best Siamese cat of the year for 1982.

In 1934, two cats were on exhibition at the Siamese Cat Club show that had white body colour, red points and blue eyes. 'Whence came the ginger?' was the comment. Dr Nora Archer and Miss A. Ray pioneered the establishing of Redpoints and Tortiepoints in the 1940s. In 1948, Dr Archer had a kitten from Mrs Lucy Price which was a Redpoint Siamese. His mother was a tortoishell bred from a Siamese queen and a red shorthair male. His father was a Sealpoint. He received from both parents the genes for the Siamese pattern restricting colour to the points, so his body was white and his points red. He was called Somerville Scarlet Pimpernel. He mated a Sealpoint queen and produced a Tortiepoint named Somerville Harliquinna who was mated back to her father, and Somerville Golden Seal, a Redpoint female, resulted. Dr Archer back-crossed Redpoint to Sealpoint to improve type.

Miss Ray had a Tortiepoint from Dr Archer and mated her to a Sealpoint to get a Redpoint male which she then mated back to his mother, producing a Redpoint female. Miss Ray bred five generations of like-to-like matings; each generation had the Siamese coat pattern. She then applied to the GCCF for a breed number, with recognition as Siamese. This was refused. Miss Ray rejected the suggestion that her Redpointed cats be called 'Foreign Shorthair'. A further attempt to gain recognition was made in 1958 and failed. By 1965, the Red-Point and Tortie-Point Siamese Cat Club had been founded, also the two clubs for Tabbypoints, and great interest was shown in the 'new varieties of Siamese'. Time had come to make a concerted effort to gain official recognition. This was granted in 1966, with the Tabbypoints, and the Redpoints were allocated breed number 32*a*. The Tortiepoints are 32*b* and the Creampoints are 32*c*.

Redpoints and Red Tabbypoints look

identical but are genetically different. This caused breeding problems at first. However, it was agreed that both be registered as Red Tabbypoints unless proven otherwise by their pedigree or their offspring. It was also decided to register Tabby-Tortiepoint cats under the tabby group and not the tortie group.

'Siamese' is a pattern and Siamese cats can be bred in any of the colours known to be feline. There are silver-tabby points in all colours, smokepoints, known as Shadowpoints, in all colours, chinchilla or shaded-silver, known as Tipped Siamese or Pastelpointed Siamese. It is possible to breed this group of colouring since the discovery of the Inhibitor gene. No attempt yet has been made to get these coloured Siamese officially recognized. Other new colours are cinnamonpoints, lavenderpoints and caramelpoints but so far these variations have not been developed.

The first Standard of Points for Siamese cats was drawn up in 1901 by the Committee of the newly formed Siamese Cat Club who only recognized those Siamese cats that conformed to that standard. This standard was adopted by Siamese fanciers throughout the world as the popularity of the breed spread. It was used in the United States of America until 1914 when they adopted their own standard. This first standard was for the 'Royal' Siamese or Sealpoints and was the same for the chocolate Siamese but for the colour of the body 'which is seal brown'. Over the years, it has been modified and revised to take in the new colours. In 1980, The Siamese Cat Joint Advisory Committee presented a new Standard of Points to the GCCF which was adopted and is currently in force. It defines the type more fully

and emphasizes the shape of head called for in today's Siamese cats – 'long and well proportioned, with width between the eyes, narrowing in perfectly straight lines to a fine muzzle, with straight profile, strong chin and level bite'. The head and profile should be wedge-shaped, neither round nor pointed. It also calls for a tail 'free from any kink'. Type is identical for all varieties. It sets out in detail the various colours required in all the varieties from Sealpoints to the newest of the officially recognized points colours, all with the accepted breed numbers, 24s and 32s and their extensions. The full Standard may be obtained from the Secretary of the Governing Council of the Cat Fancy.

The American Standards are basically similar to the English Standard; there are slight differences in the allocation of marks in the various US Standards – for example one body allows 20 marks for eyes and some only 16. The English Standard gives 15 for colour and 5 for shape. CFA's standard gives 10 marks for shape, size, slant and placement and 10 for colour. It also calls for a flat skull. 'In profile, a long straight line is seen from the top of the head to the tip of the nose. No bulge over eyes. No dip in nose'. 'Objections: Two plane profile'. 'Disqualifications: Any evidence of illness or poor health. Weak hind legs. Mouth breathing due to nasal obstruction or poor occlusion. Emaciation. Visible kink. Eyes other than blue, white toes and/or feet. Incorrect number of toes'.

Albino Siamese are shown in CFA but as AOV any other variety, non-championship. They are not admitted in the English show scene.

2 Shows and Show Activity

Probably the first cat show held in England was a side show at St Giles Fair, Winchester, in 1598. Prizes were given for the best ratter and for the best mouser. There were also cat shows in the 1860s in England and in the United States of America, but the first 'organized' cat show was the Crystal Palace Show held in 1871 and it was here that we have the first mention of that unnatural nightmare kind of cat, the Siamese. The Crystal Palace shows became annual affairs and soon cat shows were held in several places such as Birmingham, Edinburgh and Brighton Aquarium. In 1902, a Cat Section at the Annual Dog Show at the Old Deer Park, Richmond, attracted 300 entries. It was a tented affair with pens set on trestles. Straw was provided for bedding and earth was scattered at the back of the pen for sanitary needs. There was a ring class for neuters outside on the grass, with the cats wearing collars with long ribbon leads held by their owners; the judge, book in hand, in the centre and the public forming a ring all round.

Before 1910, The National Cat Club and The Cat Club each organized shows; each required separate registration and had its own rules. The

Supreme Gr Ch Zachary Apollo, Chocolate Tabbypoint, owned by Mr and Mrs K. Sillis and bred by Mrs Janet Lynn. Sire: Gr Ch Okesha Star Galaxy; dam: Simone Bat Cat. He has been Best in Show eight times, winning over all the other colours, has gained eleven Challenge Certificates and seven Grand Challenge Certificates, and was Best Cat 1982 at the Supreme Show.

National Cat Club said if the dam was served by two or more cats, their several names must be stated. Exhibitors were warned against 'faking' – 'exhibitors have been known to dye chins and treat white spots in the same manner'.

In 1910, the Governing Council of the Cat Fancy was founded and took over from the National Cat Club. Today all cat shows in Britain are licensed by the GCCF and must conform to its rules and regulations. Today's rules are basically unchanged but have been added to as the Cat Fancy expanded. All pedigree cats which are entered for licensed shows must be registered with the GCCF and have registered parents.

There are three types of cat shows – Exemption, Sanction and Championship. An Exemption Show is a beginner's show where a novice exhibitor may learn the basic rules. A Sanction Show is the next step and is run under the full rules of the Council. A Championship Show is the most important and attracts the greatest number of cats. Here Challenge certificates are awarded. Cats may become Champions if they are awarded three Challenge certificates at three Championship shows under three different judges.

Since 1976, the Governing Council of the Cat Fancy has organized the Supreme Show which is a qualifying show, open only to Grand Champions, Champions, Grand Premiers and Premiers, and kittens who have been placed first in their open classes at shows held within specified dates. Recently, certain concessions have been made to allow adolescents, cats that are nearly Champions, to enter the show. The manner of judging is different; it is termed 'ring judging' and is the continental European style where the cats are brought to the judge. The kittens are judged in the traditional way: the exhibits are in rows of pens in numerical order and judges and stewards walk from pen to pen. Other differences are the decorated pens and the restriction of the number of classes that an exhibit may enter. The pens of the kittens must not be decorated until judging is over. There is a special award at this show for the Best-in-Show Exhibit, a Supreme Championship certificate giving the title for all time of Supreme Champion or Supreme Premier. This award counts toward Grand Champion or Grand Premier status according to previous wins. A special certificate is also awarded to the Supreme Kitten to commemorate the win.

Most shows are all-breed shows but some of the specialist clubs run shows exclusively for their own breeds. The first specialist show in Britain for Siamese cats was organized in 1924 by the Siamese Cat Club in London. Cat shows in Britain are one day events whereas in Europe they can be one, two or even three day events and in the United States of America, they can be very complicated affairs indeed; sometimes four 'rings' taking place at the same time, under the same roof and with the same cats competing. There are six specialist Siamese cat shows spaced out during the Show Season held in varying locations.

There is always a health hazard in showing cats and kittens but every possible precaution is taken to minimize risks. Each exhibit is 'vetted-in' before it may be penned and any suspect is sent home or hospitalized in a special place in the show hall. It is now compulsory for an exhibit to have a current vaccination certificate against feline infectious enteritis.

Cats compete on the basis of breed, colour, sex and whether they have been neutered or not. There are separate classes for kittens and neuters. In the Siamese cat fancy, each colour variety has a separate open class; these are the most important classes and are usually judged first. Cats are 'adult' when they reach nine months old. For Siamese kittens, in the majority of the Siamese club shows the qualifying age is four to nine months. There are other classes such as Breeders class, Novice class and Club classes. Awards are given for First, Second,

Gr Ch Maeprest Stardust, Sealpoint, owned by Mrs M. Webb and bred by Mr and Mrs M.P. Williams. Sire: Ch Vaillencourt Solomon; dam: Whiterose Cleopatra. She is going a little dark with age, but still shows good contrast. She has a long, straight head, good eye colour and shape, and large well-set eyes. She is marvellous type with a delightful temperament.

Overleaf Three Sumfun Sealpoint kittens: Socrates, Jamie and Cateena. Sire: Stonecroft Coriander; dam: Sumfun Soraya.

The culmination of the show is the awarding of Best Exhibit. Each judge may nominate a cat or a kitten to 'go up' for Best-in-Show. If it has been placed first in the open class, it may go before a panel of five senior judges. At specialist Siamese shows, Best-in-Show procedure is relatively simple. The panel decides by a paper vote which is the best of all the male cats, then the females, whatever colour; then the better of the male or female. The same procedure goes for the kittens and then the best adult is assessed against the best kitten to give Best Exhibit in Show. After the decisions have been made, the names, not merely numbers, of the winning exhibits are announced and they are put into special Best-in-show pens for all to admire.

The show scene in the United States of America is vast; there are hundreds of clubs, every club throughout the USA is affiliated with one of the many cat associations and when a club puts on a show, it is sponsored by the club's affiliate, so rules and standards may differ slightly from show to show. The Siamese show world flourishes but there are few specialist shows for Siamese only, as they are known in Britain.

It all began on a very hot day in May 1885, when an Englishman, Mr James T. Hyde, organized a Cat Show in Madison Square Garden, New York. 176 cats exhibited by 125 owners endured the heat and the show was a great success. In 1898, Milwaukee, Wisconsin held a cat show and an all-pet exhibition. In 1899 a real show was held in Chicago. With the formation of the Beresford Cat Club, show activity gained momentum and many various breeds including Siamese were exhibited. Cats sent from England formed the foundation on which the American fanciers have built so well.

In 1906, Louis Wain, one-time president of Britain's National Cat Club and a committee member of the Siamese Cat Club, was judging at the Beresford Club Show in Chicago,

Third and Reserve and the appropriate prize card is placed on the exhibit's pen. Some clubs give nominal prize money and others give rosettes for the awards in the open classes.

Each exhibit has a number on a tally fastened around the neck with white ribbon or elastic and is in a pen, with the corresponding number, in a line of pens. This number is the exhibit's identity number and will be entered in the judging book and all the record books of that show.

Before judging begins, the hall will be cleared and only judges with their stewards will be allowed near the exhibits. Each cat or kitten is assessed in turn, outside the pen, on a table or trolley and the judgment recorded on duplicated slips in the judge's book. When all the exhibits entered in that particular class have been placed, one slip will go to the Show Secretary's table, one to the Award Board for the exhibitor and public to see and one stays in the judge's book.

and startled the cat world by making Lockhaven Elsa, a Sealpoint Siamese, 'Best Cat, 1906'.

In 1949, at the 33rd Championship Show of the Empire Cat Club, New York City, another English judge, the late Mr Brian Stirling-Webb, was officiating. In his review, written for one of our own magazines, he says 'The best cat I handled was Mrs Virginia Cobb's sealpoint female, Champion Newton's Jay Tee. This is a remarkable old lady (I refer to the cat, and not to Mrs Cobb) of eight who looks like a beautiful young thing of no more than two years. She has neither coarsened nor lost type in any way and is a great credit to her parents, Champion Oriental Nanki Pooh and Champion Wivenhoe Tarn, both imported from England. The best sealpoint male was H.R.H. of Ebon Mask a small but refined cat, full of type. I discovered that his dam is Doneraile Drusilla exported by Mrs Frank Williams and owned by Mr and Mrs Sven Nelson. Drusilla has been a big winner in the USA. The winner of the sealpoint female open class was another lovely cat and the only one to possess the ideal pale body colour with really dense points. She belongs to Mrs Lucas Combs of Lexington, Kentucky, but she was bred by Mrs Sayers from Oriental Silky Boy and Southwood Trinket. The best bluepoint was also from this country, Mrs Alexander Pinney's Kaybee Mia Lescula (bred by our Miss Kennedy Bell) a cat of excellent type and beautiful colour. Incidentally American bluepoints are superior to ours in the matter of colour. Their points are much bluer than those of many over here (which are frequently grey). Another thing which was very noticeable was the elegant legs and feet which are the general rule over there.'

English cats continued to cross the Atlantic; in 1960 one of the author's Siamese kittens Sumfun Banhari went to Mr John Dawe (now a CFA Judge) in California and with several English cats, Wayfarer's Sprite, Whiteoaks Mary,

Niad Si'muang, helped to found the Dahin line of Siamese. In 1965 Sumfun Shweli went to Mrs Vicky Markstein and is the great grandmother of Grand Champion Petmark Jigger.

In 1977, Lalinda's Lady Jane, a descendant of Sumfun Banhari, came from California to join her Sumfun relations in Haslemere, England. Jane's pedigree shows many eminent American bloodlines: New Moon Eclipses of Roger's Heights, Maloja's Mr B., Fan-T-Cee's Tee Cee, Singa Symphony, Che-Ree Blue Charade, Siamews Blue Cavalier of Che-Ree, Sand n' Seas Bonnie Blue of Sia-mews, Dulce Domum's Kublah of Dinapoli, all Grand Champions. Jane's sire is Champion Sin-Chiang's Montray of Lalinda and her dam is Grand Champion Lalinda's Mariah. Jane is the dam of Sumfun James Trueman, who is the sire of Sumfun Soraya.

In 1982, Sumfun Huang Feihu and Sumfun Hsi Wangmu (Sire Sumfun James Trueman) were taken to Canada and are winning prizes there; in this case American bloodlines are returning across the Atlantic, and back to the CFA show bench!

3 Breeding

If you wish to breed Siamese kittens, be sure that your queen comes from good healthy stock. Find out if her mother has a good breeding record, rearing healthy kittens. Do not breed from a queen who has obvious faults such as white toes or a kinked tail, or is in any way sub-standard. Health and a good temperament are far more important than success on the show bench, in fact many 'show' cats have proved to be poor breeders. Aim high and try to breed something that is one step nearer to perfection than your starting point.

Siamese can come into season as young as four months but do not mate your queen until she is at least ten months old, unless holding her back is obviously harming her. They can be very noisy when in season and will do all they can to get out. You will know when she is coming into season – she will become restless and fussy, rolling from side to side and rubbing around your ankles, around table legs and other objects; and some queens will 'spray'. Soon she will start to yowl. Before she is mated be sure she is in good health, on a good balanced diet, free from parasites such as fleas and worms and up to date with vaccinations. She should go to the stud about the second or third day of calling. After she has been mated, keep her quiet for a few days and do not let her out until she has finished her call. If the mating has been successful you may notice that her nipples get larger and pinker about three weeks after mating. At about five weeks you will notice a definite plumpness.

The pregnant queen should be allowed to lead a normal life; do not overfeed her but give her good quality, varied meals with perhaps additional small milky meals and vitamins.

Pregnancy is nine weeks, or about 65 days, but this can vary by two or three days either way. The days are counted from the first mating. As the birth date nears the queen will get restless, seeking out possible nesting places. She should be given a comfortable maternity box in a quiet place where she will not be harassed by other animals or humans, and where she will be warm and out of draughts. A clean cardboard box at least 24 × 18 inches and 18 inches high is ideal. Cut a door out of one side leaving a 4 inch sill. Fit this box into a second box turned on its side to form a hood. If access to the queen is necessary her box can be pulled out of the hood.

Make a 'mattress' of several layers of newspapers in an old pillowslip to fit the bottom of the box. Put several layers of sheeting on top of the mattress and a similar layer of sheeting under the mattress. When the time comes to remove the soiled bedding, slip out the mattress and top cover, leaving the queen and kittens on the clean sheeting underneath. Put the box out of direct light and keep the kittens in semi-darkness for the first two weeks.

When the queen goes into her box and purrs loudly then you can be sure the kittens are on their way. Some Siamese queens like their owner to be near at hand, but do not interfere

Beaumaris Sai Sawat, owned and bred by Brian and Anne Gregory. She is sister to Ch Beaumaris Alexander, also illustrated in this book.

unless the cat is distressed, since most queens can produce their litter without aid. This first stage may be brief or it may last for some hours. The second stage begins with visible contractions; the presenting part is now in the pelvic inlet and usually the first kitten will be born after about an hour. Normally a 'bubble' appears and the head can be seen; a strong contraction and the head is born, followed quickly by the rest of the body. The queen will break the sac and vigorously wash the kitten with her tongue to get it going; a lusty kitten will protest loudly. The placenta will follow the kitten and the mother will bite through the umbilical cord and proceed to eat the placenta. When all the kittens have been born the queen will settle down happily to feed them. Give her a bowl of warm milk with the yoke of an egg and some glucose beaten in. Do not interfere or handle the kittens if all appears well; all that is needed now is warmth, peace and quiet. Do not bother to renew the bedding until the queen voluntarily leaves the nest.

Some births are not straightforward – instead of the head presenting it may be a breech birth or tail first. Unless the queen is distressed don't worry. If she is having strong contractions and making no progress and wants to walk around the room, advice should be sought. There may be a dead kitten or an over-large one and if she has been labouring for a long time the queen will be getting exhausted. Skilled veterinary aid may be needed, sometimes a Caesarian section is necessary, but most Siamese queens are good mothers and will manage the birth calmly and sensibly.

If the queen does not release the kitten from the sac and immediately get it going, the owner must do this, clearing the mouth and nostrils and rubbing the kitten vigorously with a rough towel. Sometimes the mother does not sever the cord and you may have to do it for her. It may be cut with sterilized scissors about one inch from the body, or you may pinch the cord

between the finger and thumb of both hands. Pinch not too close to the kitten's body, keeping the hand on the kitten side steady and break the cord on the placenta side. A hot-water bottle, preferably a stone one, well wrapped up, is a comfort for the first kittens, while the mother is still busy giving birth. If the mother has eaten the placentas she may not be interested in food for the first day. She should have plenty to drink and light food such as fish, rabbit, chicken and milky foods, placed where she can eat it if she wishes. Handle the kittens as little as possible if all appear to be thriving and do not turn them into a peep-show.

Siamese kittens are born white. At about a month old colour shows on the nose and the edge of the ears, and gradually the markings or points develop. It is sometimes difficult to decide which colour the points will be, especially with the paler colours, until they are about six or seven weeks old. The eyes of Siamese kittens open early, some on the fourth or fifth day. The mother's licking will usually keep the eyes clean, but if there is stickiness bathe them very gently with boiled warm saline and encourage the mother to lick the eyelids. If they are not fully open and clean by the eighth day consult your veterinary surgeon. At about three weeks old the kittens will begin to venture out of the nest and will soon be ready for house-training. It is a good plan to restrict them to a play-pen, open at the top for the mother to get in and out freely, until they are house-trained. Do not restrict them once they are trained, as 'caging' has a bad effect on temperament. The sanitary tray should be large enough for two or three kittens to use at the same time. Use torn up tissues or lavatory paper at first, leaving a little soiled paper in the pan as a hint to the slow learners. From about the fourth week, kittens need a rough flooring such as canvas or carpeting, not a highly polished or shiny surface, so that they can run about without skidding and develop muscle tone.

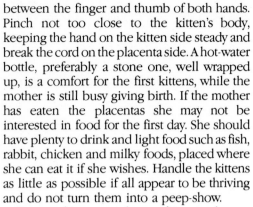

Ch Zachary Bat Girl and kittens.

Simone Bat Cat, Tabbypoint, owned by Mrs Janet Lynn and bred by Mr and Mrs J. Summerfield. Sire: Ch Simone Zeberdee; dam: New Moon Pandora.

Ch Zachary Bat Girl, Lilac Tabbypoint, bred and owned by Mrs Janet Lynn. Sire: Moondance Tanunda; dam: Simone Bat Cat.

Ch Beaumaris Alexander, Sealpoint, owned and bred by Brian and Anne Gregory. Sire: Ch Killdown Midas; dam: Karibur Justina.

Soon they will begin to show an interest in the mother's food. Weaning should be a gradual process. Start with milky foods; evaporated milk or goat's milk, if available, is better than cow's milk. Powdered baby foods may be used. Thicken the milk with baby rice or baby groats. Milk puddings, egg custard, yoghurt and cottage cheese give variety. Progress to solids, fish such as plaice, or whiting, steamed with a smear of margarine, finely cut cooked rabbit, chicken, scraped raw beef. Add a very small amount of cereal such as boiled rice, wheat flakes, wholemeal bread crumbs and cooked, mashed vegetables such as potatoes, carrots, greens, to the solid meals. Accustom the kittens to a good varied diet, but remember it should be high in protein. Try and feed each kitten separately and give only small amounts. They should have four meals a day given at regular intervals, two of them solid and two milky. Water should always be available. A pinch of veterinary bonemeal should be sprinkled on the food, also one or two vitamin

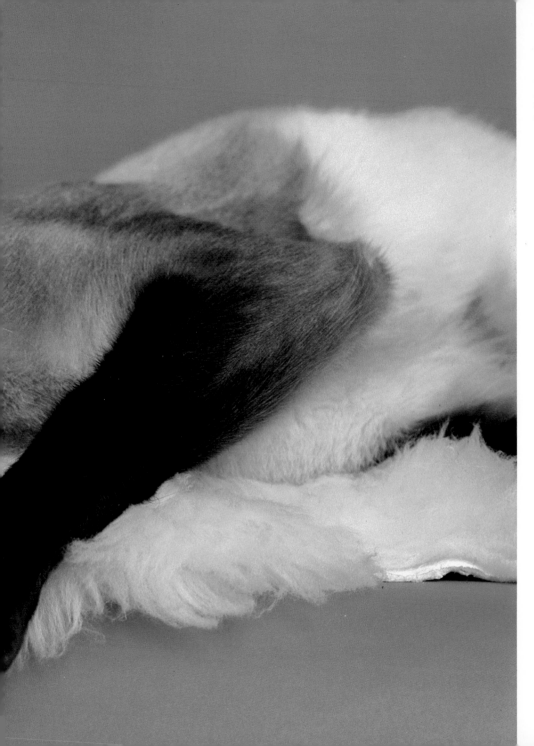

Gr Ch Amberseal Electo, Sealpoint, owned by Mrs Joan Grabham and bred by Mrs J. Walker. Sire: Gr Ch Penyrallt Picasso; dam: Chundaw Kali.

Gr Ch Shandean Dominique, Sealpoint, owned by Mrs Joan Grabham and bred by Mrs D. and Miss S. Darlow. Sire: Gr Ch Amberseal Electo; dam: Pengelly Serena.

drops. Increase the amount of food given as the kittens grow. Don't overfeed, but don't let them grow 'scrawny'.

If a male kitten is to become a stud it is best to accustom him to his own quarters from about six months. Start him with a little daily until by about nine months old he is spending all day and night in his house. Give him plenty of attention and affection, daily grooming, a good varied diet, fresh clean water and access to grass. His quarters should be dry, warm and large enough for exercise, with free access to an outdoor wired-in pen, large enough for him to run, being part grass, part stone slabs or breeze blocks, with tree trunks to climb and strop on, and shelves for sunbathing. His house must be large enough to accommodate a pen or cage for the visiting queen and this must be big enough to take her bed, drinking bowl and sanitary tray and leave ample room for movement. The stud cat sprays a lot and absorbent surfaces should be minimal. Beds can be cardboard boxes, which are renewed frequently. Some form of heating is necessary. If electricity is used it should be thermostatically controlled and so sited that the cat cannot bite any wires or burn himself. It is most important to have a porch or double door type of access to prevent the escape of visiting queens; never take chances with other people's cats.

Stud work should never be undertaken lightly, and only by the true cat lover with a gift for handling Siamese. Much time, patience and a quiet manner are necessary, and a proper sense of responsibility. Always examine a visiting queen carefully; if she has running eyes, a cold, dirty ears, or fleas or appears run down do not accept her. There is always the risk that visitors will bring an infection into your cattery. If all is well, put the queen into her own compartment and let her get to know the stud cat through the separating wire. She will probably spit at him at first, but later will croon and answer him. When she is ready, let her out to the stud; if she is willing he will mount her, grasping her by the scruff. When he has mated her she will squeal and he will jump quickly to safety. Sometimes the queen will lash out at the stud and then start to roll from side to side. *Never* attempt to touch the queen until she calms down. When she is quiet return her to her own quarters. If difficulties arise it is better to remove the stud and not to handle the queen, leaving her until you can entice her back with some food. A copy of the stud cat's pedigree should be handed to the queen's owner, with a signed statement of the dates of service. If there are no kittens from the service, it is usual to give a free mating on the queen's next call.

4 A Note on Genetics

Genetics is the science of breeding. It is the study of heredity and variation and gets more and more complicated as its development advances, and it is developing all the time. However, a knowledge of the basic principles should be sufficient for the majority of cat breeders.

Life begins with the union of a female cell, the ovum, with a male cell, the sperm, within the body of the female where it grows in an orderly manner, by the process of cell division, into an embryo and then into a foetus made up of millions of cells. It has been estimated that in the cat it may be about ten billion cells.

Ova and sperm are known collectively as gametes and the new cell formed by the union of the gametes is called a zygote. Each cell is made up of two parts, the cytoplasm and within the cytoplasm the nucleus. When the two gametes join, the two nuclei fuse and become one. Each nucleus carries the material transmitting hereditary characteristics from the parents, thus the zygote receives characteristics from the male and from the female. The zygote divides into two cells, the two cells divide to become four and so on to maturity. This process of cell division is called mitosis.

The first stage in the division of the cell is the division of the nucleus. Within the nucleus are a number of thread-like bodies called chromosomes which occur in pairs and there are several pairs in each nucleus. All the cells of all the individuals in any given species carry the same number of pairs of chromosomes. The

species we are now considering is the cat who has nineteen pairs.

The chromosomes differ from one another in size and shape, but, with certain exceptions, occur in identical pairs called homologous pairs. During mitosis each individual chromosome splits into identical halves which travel to opposite ends of the cell and by a self-copying process form two new nuclei. After mitosis both new daughter cells have sets of chromosomes identical with the mother cell and this chromosome identity is maintained in every cell of the body.

It is the chromosome that is of great importance to the breeder. Along their length the chromosomes carry minute bodies called genes which are arranged in order, one behind the other like beads on a string. The position which a gene occupies is known as its 'locus'. Each gene on the chromosome has a partner at the same position on the other chromosome of the pair. Genes related in this way are called alleles or allelomorphs. These genes are all different and are the units of heredity passed by the parents to their offspring. They control the growth and development of the fertilized egg into a whole organism. A huge number of genes is needed to embody the characteristics of an individual creature. The set of genes that an individual inherits from its parents is termed its genotype. Its physical characteristics which we actually see are called the phenotype.

Mendel, in his experiments with peas, established the laws of inheritance, working

Sumfun James Trueman sunning himself: note the clear contrast between points and body colour. Bib, chest and belly are to be pale. He has no dark spot on the stomach, and so conforms to the CFA Standard.

with one characteristic, or gene, at a time. He crossed true-breeding tall garden peas with true-breeding dwarf peas, the result was hybrids – all tall. The hybrids when mated amongst themselves produced talls and dwarfs in the proportion of 3 to 1. The dwarfs were tested and found to breed true. The talls were also tested and one-third were found to breed true to tallness whereas the other two-thirds behaved like their hybrid parents and produced three talls to one dwarf. Working similarly with green and yellow pea seeds and smooth and wrinkled pea seeds, the results were the same, that is hybrids showing only one of the characters of the pair. The other character seemed to have been lost, yet when the hybrids were crossed, the 'lost' character reappeared showing that it was not lost but only masked by the other. The character that appeared in the hybrids (the tallness, yellowness, smoothness) was called dominant and the 'lost' or hidden character was called recessive.

The phenomenon of dominance and recessiveness normally occurs only with corresponding pairs of genes (alleles). An individual inherits a pair of genes for one particular characteristic from each parent; if both members of the inherited pair are identical, the animal is said to be homozygous or true-breeding for that particular characteristic. On the other hand if a pair of dissimilar alleles is inherited, the animal is said to be heterozygous for that characteristic and 'carries' the recessive gene. A heterozygous individual can pass on the recessive gene to its offspring and if this recessive gene meets a matching recessive gene passed on by the other parent, this characteristic will no longer be dominated and will show itself in the phenotype of the animal. A recessive trait can be expressed only in a homozygous individual; chance plays a part in the meeting of recessive genes but the average over a number of experiments will be in accordance with Mendel's discovery.

Genes are referred to by symbols, usually the

initial letter of the gene name. A pair of alternative genes – alleles – share the same letter, dominant genes being set in capitals, recessive genes in small letters. Many thousands of genes go to the make-up of an animal. Some work independently, some in conjunction with others, some modify others, some mask others, some mutate. There are major genes and minor genes, polygenes, dominant genes, recessive genes, incomplete dominants and double recessives. Inhibitor genes, sex-linked genes, colour-linked genes, mimic genes and lethal genes.

For the most part, the body shape and size of cats show little real variation, which implies that genetic make-up varies less than in, for example, dogs which have been selectively bred into many shapes and sizes. However, with cats, decades of selective breeding have resulted in two principal extremes in body conformation: the compact body, short legs, short tail, round-headed 'cobby' cat and the slim, lithe body, fine bones, narrow wedge-shaped head of the cats referred to as foreign.

Most of the important major genes in cats are concerned with coat colour and quality. With the exception of the sex-linkage of the orange gene O, all coat mutants are inherited independently of the colour genes; this means that all colour varieties may be found with each type of coat and each body type. Broadly speaking some colour genes are dominant, some are recessive; some have mutated and have a diluting effect; some are called incomplete dominants or recessives. All Siamese cats have genes for tabby pattern but these are only given full expression when either agouti or orange are also present. Modifying genes influence depth of colour; shades can vary between dark and light, with intermediate shades, but the strongest 'pull' is to dark shades.

The Siamese is a cat with colour restricted to the points. Genetically this is a pattern and is often called the Himalayan pattern. This pattern is found also in other small livestock and is essentially pale-coloured hair on the body with darker 'points' or extremities, nose, ears, feet and tail and blue eyes. The Siamese pattern is caused by a gene known as the Siamese gene and symbolized c^S, that is part of the albino series of alleles. The dominant member of this group is the full colour member gene C and at the other extreme is the pink-eyed true albino. The effect of the gene is to diminish the amount of pigment in the hairs and eyes. The diminishing effect depends on temperature. New-born Siamese kittens are off-white all over; gradually pigment is formed on the cooler extremities, the ears, face, legs and tail. The pattern is most readily seen in the Sealpoint, which was the first variety to be developed. The seal colour is produced by the effect of two Siamese genes upon the non-agouti black cat; the phenotype of the Sealpoint is readily recognized. The genotype of the true-breeding Sealpoint is $aaBBc^Sc^SDD$, that is non-agouti, black, Siamese pattern, dense pigmentation, one gene of each from father and mother.

The genotypes for all other possibilities of colours and patterns of Siamese can be worked out with the gene symbols in the same way. The greatest number of possible genotypes within a Siamese variety officially recognized for Championship honours is that within the Red Tabbypoint group, for with the differences in genotype occurring as a result of sex-linked inheritance, the number becomes 24.

The difference in type from the roundish-headed, small-eared, short-tailed, almost 'cobby' Siamese cat of the early days to the show cats of today, has been achieved by selection, step by step, in accepted Mendelian manner.

The sex of each kitten is decided by a special pair of chromosomes known as the sex chromosomes. All other chromosomes are

Sexing kittens; underneath the tail are two openings; the top one is the anus and is the same for both sexes. The lower opening is the external sex organ; in females (*right*) it is a perpendicular slit called the vulva, in males (*left*) it is a circle hiding the tip of the penis. Between the anus and the circle in the male is a small sac containing two tiny testicles. The distance between the anus of the female and the vulva is approximately half the distance between the anus and the circle of the male.

A tail kink. This was once regarded as characteristic of Siamese cats — many early imports had almost hooked tails, or even bob-tails. It is a congenital deformity. In the CFA Standard a visible kink is an outright disqualification. In the GCCF Standard it is only a 'witholding' fault for Challenge or Premier Certificates — although the Standard calls for a long and tapering tail, free from any kink.

called autosomes and each one is identical to its partner. The sex chromosomes are not identical: the female chromosome is larger than the male chromosome, and is known as the X chromosome. The male chromosome is known as the Y chromosome. Female cats produce only X chromosomes, but males produce X and Y chromosomes in equal quantities. If the female germ cell carrying an X chromosome is fertilized by a male germ cell carrying an X chromosome then the resultant kitten will be female. If, on the other hand, the female germ cell is fertilized by a male germ cell carrying a Y chromosome the kitten will have a dissimilar pair of sex chromosomes (XY) and will be male.

5 Siamese as Pets: Acquisition and Care

Siamese cats make wonderful pets, since they are highly intelligent and are readily trained. Human companionship is essential to their well-being and they thrive on love and attention. They like to be talked to and will enjoy carrying on a conversation with you, as it were. They will communicate what they want and if you don't understand them it is your fault, not theirs. They will accompany you on a walk, either 'at heel' or running ahead and playing hide and seek. They can be accustomed when young to a harness and lead and many enjoy a car ride.

They will outlast you at retrieving a ball of paper or similar plaything and will play for hours with a rabbit's foot – throwing it in the air and performing like ballet dancers.

They love warmth and sunshine but will play happily in the snow, since they are as hardy as any other cat and should not be molly-coddled. They are splendid hunters, catching rabbits, mice and rats, even snakes and regrettably birds, often leaping high and catching them in flight. They are also thieves and robbers.

It is best to have neutered cats as pets. Siamese female cats can be very noisy in season and are very clever at opening doors and windows to escape. An entire male cat is impossible in the house unless you have no sense of smell. He will stray in search of females and will come back battle-scarred from

A Zachary ballet dancer! This Tabbypoint kitten is showing the liveliness and agility typical of the breed.

encounters with rivals. A pair of Siamese cats, either neutered males or speyed females, or one of each sex, is the ideal. They are much happier and much more fun in pairs and will not be lonely and miserable if left alone or boarded out on holiday.

A female kitten can be spayed at five months old but it is better to delay the operation until a little older, remembering that it is possible that she may come into season as early as four months old. Cats may be spayed at any age but never when in season. With a male kitten it is best to wait until both testicles have descended, usually upwards of six months old.

A few words of advice would not go amiss here on acquiring a Siamese kitten. Do not buy from a pet shop, but get in touch with a breeder; visit her and the kittens in their own surroundings and still with the mother cat. Do not buy and take home a kitten you see at a show. Arrange with the breeder to keep it for another ten or so days in case it has picked up an infection at the show and then collect it from her. Kittens should be lively and ready to play, bright-eyed and with clean ears. Do not accept a kitten that has runny eyes or is sneezing and looks unthrifty. Ask if the kitten has had any illness since birth and if it has had any treatment for worms. Ask if it has been inoculated against feline infectious enteritis. Is it registered with the governing body? Without a proper registration number you cannot be certain that the pedigree of the kitten is a true one. Be sure to ask for a diet sheet so that no sudden change in food or meal-times is experienced. Leaving mother and brothers and sisters can be a terrible shock for a young kitten. Take a basket or a proper container to collect your kitten – do not carry it off in your arms.

Provide your kitten with the same sanitary arrangements to which it has been trained and make any changes gradually. Your kitten will have been trained to use a sanitary tray by the mother cat, so do not allow it to become 'dirty'.

The litter tray should always be in the same place where the kitten can find it easily and it should be kept scrupulously clean. Do not use a disinfectant that contains phenol. Common soda or soap are the safest cleaners. Keep detergents and bleaches and such chemicals well out of reach of cats.

If your kitten is lonely at first, it is sometimes a comfort to put a wrapped hot-water bottle, preferably stone, in the bed and a ticking clock under the blanket as a substitute mother. The bed should be in a quiet place and out of draughts.

Make sure your kitten understands the word 'No' and start as you mean to go on. Do not spoil your kitten and let it get out of hand. Praise and reward it when it does as you wish. Show disapproval by tone of voice and never strike a cat or hurt it physically. Siamese do not like to be laughed at and made to look foolish.

Train your kitten at an early age to wear a collar, either of elastic or having an elastic inset, with an identity disc and to walk on a harness and lead – you can then take it in the garden without fear of losing it. If you can provide a wired-in garden or a large outdoor cage so much the better. A cat flap is useful when the kitten is older, but keep your Siamese safely indoors at night. Do not allow complete freedom until your kitten knows its name and comes when you call it.

All cats like to strop and sharpen their claws. They should be trained when young to understand 'No' and provided with a log of wood or a piece of hessian wrapped around a table leg or a custom-made scratching post and not allowed to strop on furniture or the stair carpet. Do not de-claw your cat, because doing this deprives the animal of a means of defence and the ability to climb and so on. If the claws need to be clipped use special nail clippers and take care not to cut the quick – the pinkish area inside the claw.

Most Siamese love to be groomed; use a fairly stiff brush of natural bristles or a rubber

Sumfun Domingo, Chocolatepoint, owned by Mrs M. Hale and bred by the author. Sire: Sumfun James Trueman; dam: Suswa Belaya.

Three very successful neuters. Left to right, Pr Leolee Lazuli, Sealpoint. Sire: Gr Ch Baranduin Leander; dam: Nomis Milady Siam. Ch and Pr Leolee Mr Apricot, Redpoint. Sire: Gr Ch Amberseal Electo; dam: Marilane Honeydew. Pr Leolee Claudius, Bluepoint. Sire: Ch Valena Beauregard; dam: Nomis Milady Siam. All owned and bred by Mrs S.L. Jackson.

brush (not nylon and never a wire brush). Use a stroking action and alternate a sweep with the brush and a firm stroke of the hand, continuing to the tip of the tail. A final stroking with a piece of silk or a chamois leather glove gives a shining gloss to a Siamese coat. Combing with a fine steel comb will remove dead hairs and, more importantly, will remove any flea droppings and fleas that may be there. It is important to keep animals free of parasites and Siamese are as susceptible to flea infestation as any other cat. A good way of dealing with this is to put the cat in a pillow-slip containing flea powder, leaving the head outside, and rub the powder into the fur through the pillow-slip. Release the cat, then brush away all the powder from its coat. Later boil the pillow-slip. Or the cat may be sprayed with a special safe spray – taking great care that it doesn't go in the eyes and ears. It is not enough to remove the fleas from the cat; the environment must also be attended to. Fleas hatch out in the dust on floors, bedding, upholstery. Floors should be vacuumed and washed frequently. A safe flea powder is pybuthrin. Do not use any containing DDT.

Inspect the ears and wipe the flaps with a damp swab of cotton wool but *do not* poke inside. If the ears are smelly and show a dark deposit inside, seek veterinary help. If you need to bathe the eyes, use a clean swab of cotton wool soaked in warm water or saline, a separate swab for each eye. The eyelids and the nictitating membrane or haw (sometimes called the third eyelid) serve to protect the eye ball against dust and grit. If there is inflammation or a discharge, 'sticky eyes', which does not respond to a simple bathing with saline, veterinary diagnosis should be sought so that the proper remedy is prescribed. Eye drops are usually more effective than ointment and more easily applied.

Check the mouth and teeth regularly. The gums should not be red and sore, the tongue should be clean and the teeth free of tartar. In young kittens, teething may cause a sore mouth and a reluctance to eat. Massaging the gums with a little honey is a safe way of alleviating the trouble. Older cats are prone to get a tartar deposit which causes trouble. Sometimes it completely embeds the teeth and causes decay. It is best to have a veterinary surgeon clean up the mouth under anaesthetic, removing the tartar and extracting any bad teeth. The cat will manage to eat much better 'on its gums' than with tartared or bad teeth. It is as well to have the mouth checked regularly by a vet.

Cats require a diet rich in protein. Meat, including some fat, fish, offal, eggs and milk should be the mainstay with cooked vegetables and cereals. The diet should be as varied as possible and an animal should not be allowed to become habituated to one kind of food. It should consist of raw, cooked and canned items and it is important to ensure adequate water consumption. Cats need about ½ ounce per pound of bodyweight a day; an average 10 lb cat needs 5 ounces of food daily, at least 4 ounces being protein (meat or fish). Kittens should have four or five small meals a day, at regular intervals. Adult cats should be fed morning and night, with *no* tit-bits in between.

Pregnant and lactating queens need additional meals. Elderly cats and those recovering from illness should have small meals more frequently than the routine morning and night. Never give raw fish or uncooked white of egg. Give liver sparingly, add salt, preferably iodized, when cooking food. Some Siamese cannot tolerate milk because it gives them diarrhoea. Water should always be readily available. Give food at room temperature, not ice-cold from the refrigerator.

Give a good varied diet in clean dishes at regular mealtimes; don't overfeed and don't leave un-eaten food down.

You must decide for yourself whether your Siamese cat is to be allowed full freedom or if it

Sumfun Ellyamerling, Chocolatepoint, owned by Mrs M. Hale and bred by the author. Sire: Sumfun James Trueman; dam: Suswa Belaya.

are provided – warmth in winter, fresh cool air in summer, clean litter tray, water always available, and meals at regular times. Be sure your house or flat is escape-proof. Open windows can have mesh frames fitted, open fires and chimneys should be guarded. Cooking stoves and refrigerators are hazards, and disinfectants, some cleaning agents and bleaches are dangerous, while many house-plants are poisonous. Cats tend to chew greenery so provide them with a pot of grass brought in from the garden or grown from seed.

The restricted cat needs exercise and entertainment so be sure to provide plenty of playthings, ping pong balls, twists of paper, cardboard boxes, tunnels etc. and of course, best of all, a companion cat to chase and play with. If you have trained your cat to a harness and lead as a kitten you can take it for walks, but avoid busy and noisy places.

If you need to board your cat make very careful enquiries and seek recommendations from other cat owners; go and see for yourself and ask questions. Some catteries will not take an unneutered male and some will even refuse to have Siamese at all.

Siamese cats are the worst of patients; if they are ill they tend to give up more easily than others. They make better progress if they are nursed by someone they know and in their own surroundings. Quiet and rest are important and the ill cat should be disturbed as little as possible. Every effort should be made to prevent dehydration and to maintain the cat's strength. A syringe is useful for giving fluids, administered slowly into the soft pouch at the side of the mouth.

should be confined to the house or in an outside run. Free roaming cats run many risks, fights, traffic accidents, theft, infection, getting lost and becoming strays. If your Siamese has never known freedom it will be content to stay indoors but it is very important that all its needs

6 Clubs and the Cat Fancy

The Cat Fancy began, basically, when it was realized that some kind of organization was needed to regulate and control the several cat clubs and cat shows that had resulted from Harrison Weir's first Crystal Palace Show in 1871. In 1887 the National Cat Club was formed to promote the pure breeding of cats, and to keep a register of pedigree cats and to hold shows. For 11 years it was the supreme authority. In 1898, a splinter group headed by Lady Marcus Beresford founded The Cat Club with exactly the same aims. The Cat Club died in 1905 and for a while the National Cat Club reigned supreme. In 1908 there were further quarrels and breakaways and eight clubs formed their own federation called the Cat Fanciers' Association. By 1910, after much quarrelling, a conference of all parties was called and it was decided to form a Council to be called The Governing Council of the Cat Fancy. The National Cat Club agreed to hand over its governing powers to the new Council and was granted four delegates 'in perpetuity' in recompense. The new Council took over all registrations and also the granting of Championships. It held its first general meeting at the Inns of Court Hotel, London on 11 October 1910.

The Registers of the National Cat Club, the Incorporated Cat Fanciers Association and the Scottish Cat Club were incorporated with that of the GCCF. There were sixteen founder clubs listed; the oldest was the National (1887) and then the Scottish Cat Club was founded in 1894.

The Siamese Cat Club's date is given as 1900. Some of the clubs such as Wilson's Ltd Cat Club have long since disappeared.

The Council is a democratic body composed of delegates of affiliated cat clubs and societies who are elected annually by the members of those clubs. From small beginnings it has gone from strength to strength. Today, there are more than 100 affiliated clubs sending delegates to meetings. The honorary officers of the Council and the various committees within it are elected annually by the delegates from the delegate body. Four Registrars are now needed to deal with registrations and transfers, one for all the Longhair breeds, one for Shorthair and since 1962, a specialist for Siamese with more recently, one for Burmese registrations. The Council employs a Secretary to deal with general business and the volume of work today is formidable.

Council issues stud books and lists, grants licences for shows, approves standards for new varieties and publishes a book of all the standards on which the officially recognized breeds are judged. Council appoints judges to the official list from nominations sent in by the various selection bodies, such as the Siamese Cat Joint Advisory Committee.

The Siamese Cat Fancy has expanded from the original club founded in 1900 with a membership of 31. In the early days the Siamese Cat Club was omnipotent, but with the expansion of the fancy there were breakaways and today there are 13 affiliated Siamese specialist clubs, some for all colours, some for a particular colour or pattern. The larger clubs run their own specialist shows, some of the smaller clubs amalgamating to run a show.

In the United States of America the Cat Fancy dates back to about the middle of the nineteenth century. The first really professional show was inspired by those held at the Crystal Palace in England. It was held in Madison Square Gardens, New York, in 1895 and was organized by an Englishman. In 1899 the Beresford Cat Club, named after Lady Marcus Beresford who founded The Cat Club in England, was established by Mrs Clinton Locke, its first president. With this nucleus, the American Cat Association was founded in 1901 as a continent-wide registering and show-sponsoring body. From then on, several other registering bodies have branched off so that today the United States has a multifarious number of registering bodies, making an extraordinary amount of confusion, paperwork, duplication and expense. The largest is the CFA with over half the total cat fancy membership, with the ACFA well in second place. Both are continent-wide and the CFA has Japanese affiliates. The various bodies are known by their initials and in the main are regional. They have their own rules and standards of points, they appoint their own judges, they register cats and sanction shows. Most of the governing bodies recognize as Siamese the Seal-, Blue-, Chocolate- and Lilac-pointed cats but classify other colours as Colourpoint shorthairs. Some include only Red and Tortoiseshell in their Colourpoint category. One body, while recognizing officially the four basic colours including Reds and Torties, adds Albinos but omits Lynxpoints (as the Tabby-points are called). Some bodies call the Lilac-points 'Frostpoints' and the Redpoints 'Flame-points'. Standards vary in minor respects. Most of the shows are all-breed shows and there are very few for Siamese only. No kitten

may be shown under four months old and a kitten becomes a cat at eight months. The shows attract enormous 'gates' though the number of exhibits is low compared with shows in Britain.

The Cat Fancy in Canada is relatively young. The first recorded show was in 1906 in Toronto with one judge. It was an all-breed show and there were 124 entries, longhairs, shorthairs and household pets but no Siamese. Cats did not have to be registered. After the war the Canadian National Cat Club once again sponsored shows at the annual Canadian National Exhibition. The CNE Cat Show, for many years was the most important cat show in North America, with exhibitors from the United States as well as Canada. In 1968 the Canadian National Cat Club was disbanded and the sponsorship handed over to the Royal Canadian Cat Club which was affiliated with the Canadian Cat Association. The CCA was founded in 1960 and became the first registering body. Before that all cat registrations were sent to one of the American associations. The first CCA show was held in Ottawa in 1963 and now there are a number of clubs all across Canada putting on cat shows. Canada works very closely with the United States and, as well as offering its own CCA Championships and Grand Champion-ships, offers International Championships and International Grand Championships where cats must gain their Championships both under CCA rules and under the American Club's rules. The Canadian cat fancy is growing fast.

The European Cat Fancies are divided into a number of independent bodies. The largest, FIFE (Fédération Internationale Féline de l'Europe) controls a total of over 15 cat clubs operating in Austria, Belgium, Czechoslovakia, Denmark, Finland, France, Germany, Holland, Italy, Norway, Sweden and Switzerland. Each of the FIFE clubs sends a delegate to the annual general meeting which determines the overall policy. The member clubs in each country

governing body. Some clubs hold two or three championship shows in a season. For the most part the shows are run on much the same lines as in Britain and the GCCF standard of points for judging is used, with one or two minor adjustments.

Siamese are the most popular cats, with the Sealpoint in first place. All the colours are seen on the show bench and while many lines have come from imported British stock, there are many lines of several generations of purely Australian breeding. There is great interest in cat breeding and showing in Australia and Tasmania.

New Zealand has a very active Cat Fancy. Like Britain, New Zealand is controlled by one central body, the Governing Council of the Cat Fancy of New Zealand. The rules of registration, breeding and showing are similar to those of Australia. The largest show is the National Cat Show organized by a different club in a different city each year and sponsored by a pet foods firm. It attracts an entry of well over 600 exhibits of all breeds. Many of the Siamese are imports from Britain.

The Cat Fancy in South Africa got into its stride in the early 1950s. From about 1964 interest in cats has increased considerably and has been maintained. The standard of points used is the same as the British and the show rules have been based on British show rules with some modifications to suit South African requirements. The overall governing body, the Governing Council of the Associated Cat Clubs of South Africa, was formed in 1970. The clubs operate autonomously and the Council is primarily a liaison body. The delegates, one from each club, carry mandates from their respective clubs for all matters except show rules and no resolutions can be carried without reference to all clubs and a majority agreement. The South African Cat Register deals with all registrations and transfers in South Africa. The Siamese is the most popular breed.

Killdown Medea, Seal Tabbypoint and sister of Killdown Midas. Owned by Brian and Anne Gregory and bred by Mrs I. Keene.

maintain their own register of cats and issue their own pedigree certificates.

There are also a number of independent cat bodies who have formed their own registering bodies and clubs and hold their own shows. Cat shows staged in Europe are usually two-day affairs in order to allow exhibitors to come over long distances. They are very elaborate affairs with decorated pens and flower-massed halls.

Australia has seven distinct areas, each with its own cat fancy, its own cat register and its own constituted governing body. They have been based on the English systems from the beginning and their registration system, show organization and judging are remarkably uniform. Cat clubs flourish in each state and are affiliated to and controlled by their particular

Gr Ch Simone
Strawberries, Chocolate
Tabbypoint, bred and
owned by John and
Wendy Summerfield.
Sire: Ch Zaparta
Comet; dam:
Funnyface Tansie. He
has a sister called
'Raspberries'!

Ch Livrabar Strawman, Lilacpoint, bred and owned by Mr and Mrs B. Summerfield. Sire: Simone Semolina Silkpaws; dam: Ch Livrabar Savak.

The cat fancy in South Africa is very much a hobby one. Distances between show venues are long so that air transport is the order of the day. South African cats may be exhibited in Zimbabwe and vice versa, but rabies regulations and distance make this interchange difficult.

Patrician Papoose, Redpoint, owned by Mr Peter Greenaway and bred by Mrs S. Humphris. Sire: Ch Patrician Nijinsky; dam: Adonis Gold Charm.

Below Foxtwist Justine, Chocolate Tabbypoint, owned by Mrs Joan Grabham and bred by Mrs S. Spencer.

Index · Numbers in bold type refer to illustrations

For further information on clubs and societies worldwide please write to: Mrs W. Davies, The Secretary, GCCF, 'Dovefields', Petworth Road, Witley, Surrey GU8 5QW.